DESSERTS
AROUND THE
WORLD

This book is available in two editions:
Library binding by Lerner Publications Company,
    a division of Lerner Publishing Group
Soft cover by First Avenue Editions,
    an imprint of Lerner Publishing Group
241 First Avenue North
Minneapolis, MN 55401 U.S.A.

Website address: www.lernerbooks.com

Library of Congress Cataloging-in-Publication Data

Engfer, Lee
    Desserts around the world / compiled and edited by Lee Engfer.—
Rev. and updated.
      p.   cm. — (Easy menu ethnic cookbooks)
    Rev. ed. of: Desserts around the world / photographs by Robert L. and
Diane Wolfe. 1991.
    Summary: Presents recipes for making favorite desserts from around
the world and explains the traditions behind them.
    ISBN: 0–8225–4126–2 (lib. bdg. : alk. paper)
    ISBN: 0–8225–4165–3 (pbk. : alk. paper)
    1. Desserts—Juvenile literature. 2. Cookery, International—Juvenile
literature. [1. Desserts. 2. Cookery, International.] I. Engfer, Lee, 1963–
II. Series.
TX773 .D4745 2004
641.8'6—dc21   2002152935

Manufactured in the United States of America
1 2 3 4 5 6 – JR – 09 08 07 06 05 04

easy menu ethnic cookbooks

DESSERTS

revised and expanded

AROUND THE

to include new

WORLD

low-fat recipes

compiled by Lee Engfer

Lerner Publications Company • Minneapolis

Contents

Introduction

How many times have you wished you could skip the main dish and dig right into dessert? If you have a sweet tooth, you're not alone. People all over the world enjoy desserts in one form or another. And they have been doing so throughout history.

Honey was the first sweetener. An ancient cave painting in Spain shows a person under attack from bees while stealing wild honey from a hive. Egyptian tomb paintings dating from 5500 to 3000 B.C. also feature bees and honey.

Ancient Egyptians ate a confection of crushed almonds and honey. The Greeks and Romans used honey to coat fruits, flowers, and the seeds or stems of plants. In Greece cheese curds and cheesecake with honey were favorite treats. In ancient Rome, the traditional birthday cake was made of wheat flour, grated cheese, honey, and olive oil and was served with honeyed wine. In China during the tenth century, mi-king, or honey bread, was popular.

In North America, the Mohawk and Algonquian Indians also used honey in cooking. They stuffed pumpkins with honey, cider, and

Russia is one of many places where people enjoy honey-sweetened desserts. Many Russian children love this honey cake. (Recipe on page 45.)

7

Sugarcane grows best in places with warm, tropical climates. This sugarcane plantation is in Guadeloupe, in the Caribbean.

beaver fat and baked them in the embers of a fire. The native people of Canada crushed strawberries in honey to form a sweet paste that would keep through the winter months.

Other sweeteners of the ancient world included syrups made from dates and figs, grape juice, malted grains, and sugarcane juice. Sugarcane was probably first grown on the island of New Guinea in the South Pacific about eight thousand years ago. From there it spread to other Polynesian islands, then to Indonesia, the Philippines, India, and China.

According to legends in India, the ancestors of Buddha (the founder of Buddhism) came from the land of sugar, or Gur. The great Indian epic the *Ramayana*, written about 1200 B.C., describes a banquet that included "tables laid with sweet things, syrup, canes to chew."

Through invasions, conquests, and trading caravans, sugar eventually made its way throughout the Middle East and Europe. Christopher Columbus brought sugarcane to the Caribbean around 1500, and by 1600 sugar production in the Americas had become the world's largest and most profitable industry. Demand for sugar, which was considered a luxury food, fueled the slave trade and shaped the history of the New World. To meet the increasing demand, sugar plantations needed more workers—so they shipped slaves from Africa. European settlers who moved to America brought cooking skills and recipes with them and learned about new foods and ways to prepare them from Native Americans.

Changing Traditions

Until about the 1500s, most foods—not just what we think of as desserts—had honey or sugar added to them, along with spices and salt. Meats, for example, were often cooked in a heavy syrup of sugar with almonds and fruit. Early candies were a mixture of sugar and spices. Cloves, ginger, aniseed, and other spices and nuts were dipped in melted sugar and cooked in a pan. These concoctions were supposed to aid digestion.

Desserts weren't always served at the end of a meal, either. For many years, dessert was served at the same time as the meat or soup. At banquets pastries appeared on the table beside roast goat, cabbage soup, mustard, and pickled cucumbers, and people ate whatever they could reach from where they sat.

Forks weren't invented until the Renaissance, a cultural period that began in Italy in the 1300s and gradually extended throughout Europe and England. As cooking and table manners became refined, table settings and desserts became more elaborate. Dainty cakes with intricate decorations, flavored ice creams, sherbets, and pies were served. Such dishes were the beginning of modern desserts.

A World of Tasty Treats

Geography, custom, and practical use of local ingredients are all factors that influence the types of sweets people choose to eat and when they eat them. Popular desserts around the world include cakes, cookies, biscuits, ice cream, pudding, pies, and sweet breads.

In some places, however, fancy, rich desserts are uncommon. In many African and Asian countries, people rarely eat a dessert at the end of a meal. For example, dessert is not part of the traditional meal in sub-Saharan Africa (the countries south of the Sahara Desert). At large gatherings and celebrations, a fruit salad might be served after a meal. While most Africans do not eat dessert, they do enjoy some sweet snacks, such as fresh fruits, raw sugarcane, or cookies made in a pan over an open fire.

In many cultures, especially in warm and tropical climates, fresh fruit is the main dessert. In the Southeast Asian country of Thailand, for example, you may have a choice of assorted fruit, such as papaya, guava, and pineapple, at the end of a meal. But Thais also enjoy a

Fruit is a common dessert in many parts of the world. These women sell fruit at an open-air market near Bangkok, Thailand.

variety of sweet treats for snacking, which are often sold on the street. These include deep-fried bananas, coconut pudding, sweet pancakes, and sticky rice cooked in coconut milk and served with mango or other fruit.

Fruits are common dessert ingredients everywhere. Along with eggs and sugar, fruits have long been used to create a wide array of tempting desserts. Two other favorite dessert flavorings are vanilla and chocolate. The Maya and Aztec Indians in Mexico were the first people to enjoy chocolate, which was originally served as a beverage. According to an Aztec legend, the god Quetzalcoatl showed the people how to grow cacao trees, harvest their seedpods, and prepare chocolate from the seeds of the sacred tree.

Desserts may be served not only after lunch or dinner but for an afternoon coffee or tea break. In the British Isles and Australia, many people stop for tea in the late afternoon. Sometimes it can be quite a formal occasion, with a selection of small sandwiches, biscuits, and cakes, both elaborate and plain. Lamingtons (small, frosted cubes of cake covered with coconut) are a good choice for teatime, and they are a favorite with Australian children. People in Germany, Austria, the Scandinavian countries, and some Latin American countries may also take a break in the afternoon to linger over coffee and pastries.

Holidays and Festivals

Since the dawn of history, sweet foods have been served for special occasions and as part of religious rituals. In ancient funerals, the dead were given a supply of honey to enjoy in the afterlife, since honey symbolized immortality. Ancient peoples even buried important leaders in honey. In many cultures, sweets—whether honey, sugar, or chocolate—were considered the food of the gods.

Many rituals of life and nature are still celebrated with sweets. In Lebanon, for example, *meghlie*, or milk pudding, is served to visitors when a child is born. The Hopi Indians of Arizona mark the winter solstice (the shortest day of the year) with a meal containing honey and flour. And in many cultures, cake is a cornerstone of weddings and birthdays.

Throughout the world, people prepare special desserts for holidays and festivals. You could fill several cookbooks with recipes for desserts for Christmas, the major Christian holiday that celebrates the birth of Jesus. These desserts range from sweet fruit breads—such as the *pan de Navidad* in Chile, three kings bread in Mexico, and the *Julebrød* in Norway—to dozens of types of cookies to Mexican fried pastries (*buñelos*) to Scandinavian rice pudding to special cakes such as the *bûche de Noël* (yule log) in France.

Desserts are also an important part of many Jewish holidays. At Rosh Hashanah, the high holy days that begin the Jewish New Year, the table is laid with symbolic foods, including new fruits of the season such as pomegranates, figs, persimmons, apples, and pears. Bowls of honey symbolize the wish for a sweet year. Delicious cookies filled with poppy seeds or fruit are served during Purim. This holiday celebrates the story of Queen Esther of Persia, who helped bring down the wicked Haman, who had planned to kill all Jews living in Persia. The pastries, called Haman's pockets or Haman's ears (*hamantaschen*), are shaped like Haman's three-cornered hat.

Many Hindu holidays would not be complete without a table full of different types of sweets. Desserts for Diwali (the Hindu festival of lights) include *kheer*, a sweet rice pudding prepared with rice, milk, nuts, and spices; halva, a rich blend of butter, grated vegetables, chopped nuts, honey, and dried fruit; and *thandi*, a nutty, spicy milk shake. The Holi festival—celebrating the arrival of spring—features *puran poli*, sweet stuffed bread, and *gujjia*, deep-fried pastries filled with nuts or raisins.

Ramadan is the most important holiday for followers of Islam. During this holy month, Muslims fast (neither eating nor drinking) from sunup to sundown and eat simple meals before dawn and after dark. A celebration called Eid al-Fitr marks the end of Ramadan and is celebrated with a lavish feast, complete with a variety of sweet

An Indian girl lights a special lamp in celebration of the Hindu festival of Diwali.

dishes. In Lebanon pancakes stuffed with sugared nuts and drenched in sweet syrup are eaten at this time.

Many festivals across the globe celebrate the changing seasons, the New Year, the harvest, or a particular food. In Sweden Midsummer Eve marks the summer solstice—the longest day of the year. At this magical time of year, the twilight lasts until eleven at night, and dawn breaks at 2:00 A.M. Families and friends gather to decorate a maypole with birch leaves and wildflowers. They dance, sing, and feast on pickled herring, new potatoes, and desserts made with strawberries, such as *jorbgubbstårta*, the Swedish version of strawberry shortcake.

The strawberry is also the star of the Festival of Strawberries in

Nemi, Italy, a town near Rome. Strawberries grow in abundance on the hillsides surrounding Nemi, and on a Sunday in June, townspeople parade around dressed as ancient strawberry pickers or even as the berries themselves. People eat the freshly picked berries plain or with cream and sugar.

Harvest festivals for many different foods take place throughout the world. In the African countries of Ghana and Nigeria, for example, a yam festival is held around the beginning of August, as the first yam crops are harvested. Yams, which are similar to sweet potatoes, are a major part of the diet in many African countries. Besides being eaten as a main dish, they may be fried and sprinkled with sugar and cinnamon for a sweet snack.

In China special sweet cakes are prepared for the New Year festivities. The date of Chinese New Year changes each year because it falls on the first day of the lunar calendar, which is based on the phases

This family's Chinese New Year dinner includes oranges, which traditionally symbolize good fortune.

of the moon. The New Year season is also called the Spring Festival. People decorate their homes with red paper and set off firecrackers. The season ends with a colorful Lantern Festival. The New Year is celebrated with many festive foods, including desserts.

Many other worldwide holidays feature desserts. In Mexico people honor the dead during the Day of the Dead holiday. This is not a somber occasion but a festive time filled with flowers, candles, and special foods, including a sweet bread called *pan de muertos* (bread of the dead). A similar holiday in Italy is celebrated with "dead bone cookies"—crunchy cookies that resemble bones.

Australians pay tribute to people who died in war on Anzac Day, April 25. ANZAC stands for Australian and New Zealand Army Corps. Anzac biscuits—crisp coconut cookies—were baked for ANZAC soldiers during World War I (1914–1918) and World War II (1939–1945).

In every corner of the world, people find pleasure in the sweet delights of desserts, from simple fruits to elaborate cakes and pastries. The recipes in this book are from around the globe. By making all the recipes, you can sample some of the best treats the world has to offer.

Before You Begin

Cooking any dish, plain or fancy, is easier and more fun if you are familiar with its ingredients. Some dessert recipes make use of ingredients that you may not know. Sometimes special cookware is also used, although the recipes in this book can easily be prepared with ordinary utensils and pans.

The most important thing you need to know before you start is how to be a careful cook. On the following page, you'll find a few rules that will make your cooking experience safe, fun, and easy. Next, take a look at the "dictionary" of cooking utensils, terms, and special ingredients. You may also want to read the tips on preparing healthy, low-fat desserts.

Once you've picked out a recipe to try, read through it from beginning to end. Now you are ready to shop for ingredients and to organize the cookware you will need. When you have assembled everything, you're ready to begin cooking.

This Greek yogurt pie is a sweet treat that contains healthy ingredients such as ricotta cheese, yogurt, and fruit. (Recipe on page 44.)

The Careful Cook

Whenever you cook, there are certain safety rules you must always keep in mind. Even experienced cooks follow these rules when they are in the kitchen.

- Always wash your hands before handling food. Thoroughly wash all raw vegetables and fruits to remove dirt, chemicals, and insecticides. Wash uncooked poultry, fish, and meat under cold water.
- Use a cutting board when cutting up vegetables and fruits. Don't cut them up in your hand! And be sure to cut in a direction *away* from you and your fingers.
- Long hair or loose clothing can easily catch fire if brought near the burners of a stove. If you have long hair, tie it back before you start cooking.
- Turn all pot handles toward the back of the stove so that you will not catch your sleeves or jewelry on them. This is especially important when younger brothers and sisters are around. They could easily knock off a pot and get burned.
- Always use a pot holder to steady hot pots or to take pans out of the oven. Don't use a wet cloth on a hot pan because the steam it produces could burn you.
- Lift the lid of a steaming pot with the opening away from you so that you will not get burned.
- If you get burned, hold the burn under cold running water. Do not put grease or butter on it. Cold water helps to take the heat out, but grease or butter will only keep it in.
- If grease or cooking oil catches fire, throw baking soda or salt at the bottom of the flame to put it out. (Water will *not* put out a grease fire.) Call for help, and try to turn all the stove burners to "off."

Cooking Utensils

double boiler—Two saucepans that fit together so that the contents of the upper pan can be cooked or heated by boiling water in the bottom pan. If you don't have a double boiler, you can improvise by placing a heatproof mixing bowl over a larger pot filled with water.

electric mixer—An appliance, either freestanding or handheld, used for mixing and beating

food processor—An electric appliance with a blade that revolves inside a container to chop, mix, or blend food

springform pan—A pan with a detachable rim

whisk—A wire utensil for beating foods by hand

zester—A tool that peels off the rind of citrus fruits in thin strips

Cooking Terms

beat—To stir rapidly in a circular motion

blanch—To submerge a food in boiling water for a short time

core—To remove the core (the inedible central part) from a fruit

cream—To beat two or more ingredients (such as butter and sugar) together until the mixture has a creamy consistency

dice—To chop food into small cubes

fold—To blend an ingredient with other ingredients by using a gentle overturning circular motion instead of by stirring or beating

garnish—To add a decorative touch

hull—To remove the hull (inedible outer covering) from a fruit

mince—To chop food into very fine pieces

pinch—A very small amount, usually what you can pick up between your thumb and forefinger preheat—To allow an oven to warm up before putting food into it

puree—To mash to a smooth blend or make a paste or thick liquid from finely ground food. The mashed substance is also referred to as a puree.

separate—To divide one ingredient into two or more parts that will be used separately, such as egg yolk and egg white

sift—To mix several dry ingredients together or to remove lumps in dry ingredients by putting them through a sieve or sifter

simmer—To cook over low heat in liquid kept just below its boiling point. Bubbles may occasionally rise to the surface.

whip—To beat an ingredient, such as cream or egg whites, at high speed until light and fluffy

whisk—To beat with a whisk until well mixed

Special Ingredients

brown candy—A hard form of dark sugar available in packages or sometimes sold in bulk at specialty markets

cardamom—A spice from the ginger family that has a rich aroma and gives food a sweet, cool taste

cinnamon—A spice made from the bark of a tree in the laurel family. It is available ground and in sticks.

cloves—The highly fragrant dried flower buds of a tropical tree of the myrtle family, used whole or ground as a spice

cocoa—Powdered, ground, roasted cacao beans from which some fat has been removed. The chocolate powder is often used in baking.

coconut milk—A smooth, rich-flavored liquid made from coconuts that is used in soups, sauces, curries, and desserts. Reduced-fat (light) coconut milk is available and can be substituted for regular coconut milk in recipes.

dates—Small brown fruits of the tropical palm tree with very sweet, tender flesh. They are often dried and used for eating and cooking.

glutinous rice flour—A powder made from sweet or glutinous rice, available at most specialty stores. Also called sticky rice flour or sweet rice flour, this is different from regular rice flour and the two can not be substituted for each other.

mango—A greenish yellow tropical fruit with soft, juicy, yellow flesh

nutmeg—A fragrant spice, either whole or ground, that is often used in desserts

orange flower water—A liquid flavoring made from distilled orange blossoms

papaya—A pear-shaped tropical fruit with golden-yellow skin and juicy, sweet yellow flesh

pistachios—Small, greenish nuts from an Asian tree of the cashew family

ricotta cheese—A soft, creamy, light-colored cheese similar to cottage cheese. It may be made from whole or skim milk.

sticky rice—A type of rice that is sticky or glutinous when cooked. It is different from regular long- or medium-grain rice and is sold in Asian grocery markets.

sweetened condensed milk—Whole milk from which half the water has been evaporated and to which sugar has been added. It is heated, cooled, and canned.

yeast—An ingredient used in baking that causes dough to rise

Healthy and Low-Fat Cooking Tips

Many cooks are concerned about preparing healthy, low-fat meals. Desserts present a special challenge, since many sweet dishes are made with butter, milk, cream, and other high-fat dairy products. Fortunately, there are simple ways to reduce the fat content of most desserts. Throughout the book, you'll also find specific suggestions for adapting individual recipes—and don't worry, they'll still taste delicious!

One of the best ways to cut down on fat in desserts is to choose fruit-based recipes. Fruit is naturally low in fat and calories—and is packed with vitamins and other nutrients. When a recipe calls for butter, you may be able to use oil or margarine instead. Before making such a substitution, consider the recipe. The taste or consistency of many desserts may noticeably change if you substitute margarine or oil for butter.

When making baked goods, you can often substitute applesauce for part of the fat content. For example, in a recipe that calls for ½ cup oil, you can replace half the oil with applesauce. Other good substitutions are pureed squash, apricots, or prunes or cooked, grated beets. These ingredients add moistness without adding fat.

Omitting egg yolks reduces the fat in recipes considerably. Lightly beaten egg whites can replace some or all of the eggs in most recipes. In general, you can replace 1 large egg with 2 egg whites and 2 medium eggs with 3 egg whites. Egg substitutes are also available.

An easy way to trim fat from a recipe is to use skim milk or buttermilk in place of cream or whole milk. Buttermilk, like skim milk, is low in fat. In baked goods, for every cup of buttermilk you use add ½ tsp. of baking soda to the dry ingredients.

In recipes that call for sour cream, you can substitute low-fat or nonfat yogurt. Another way to reduce fat is to use part-skim ricotta cheese in place of regular ricotta. Coconut milk, used in many Asian recipes, is available in "light" versions that are lower in fat. Low-fat or nonfat nondairy toppings can be substituted for whipping cream.

Finally, a simple way to reduce fat is simply to cut about 25 percent of the fat in a recipe and increase the liquid content slightly. It may take some experimenting to get the proportions right.

There are many ways to prepare desserts that are good for you and still taste great. As you become a more experienced cook, try experimenting with recipes and substitutions to find the methods that work best for you.

METRIC CONVERSIONS

Cooks in the United States measure both liquid and solid ingredients using standard containers based on the 8-ounce cup and the tablespoon. These measurements are based on volume, while the metric system of measurement is based on both weight (for solids) and volume (for liquids). To convert from U.S. fluid tablespoons, ounces, quarts, and so forth to metric liters is a straightforward conversion, using the chart below. However, since solids have different weights—one cup of rice does not weigh the same as one cup of grated cheese, for example—many cooks who use the metric system have kitchen scales to weigh different ingredients. The chart below will give you a good starting point for basic conversions to the metric system.

MASS (weight)

1 ounce (oz.)	=	28.0 grams (g)
8 ounces	=	227.0 grams
1 pound (lb.) or 16 ounces	=	0.45 kilograms (kg)
2.2 pounds	=	1.0 kilogram

LIQUID VOLUME

1 teaspoon (tsp.)	=	5.0 milliliters (ml)
1 tablespoon (tbsp.)	=	15.0 milliliters
1 fluid ounce (oz.)	=	30.0 milliliters
1 cup (c.)	=	240 milliliters
1 pint (pt.)	=	480 milliliters
1 quart (qt.)	=	0.95 liters (l)
1 gallon (gal.)	=	3.80 liters

LENGTH

¼ inch (in.)	=	0.6 centimeters (cm)
½ inch	=	1.25 centimeters
1 inch	=	2.5 centimeters

TEMPERATURE

212°F	=	100°C (boiling point of water)
225°F	=	110°C
250°F	=	120°C
275°F	=	135°C
300°F	=	150°C
325°F	=	160°C
350°F	=	180°C
375°F	=	190°C
400°F	=	200°C

(To convert temperature in Fahrenheit to Celsius, subtract 32 and multiply by .56)

PAN SIZES

8-inch cake pan	=	20 x 4-centimeter cake pan
9-inch cake pan	=	23 x 3.5-centimeter cake pan
11 x 7-inch baking pan	=	28 x 18-centimeter baking pan
13 x 9-inch baking pan	=	32.5 x 23-centimeter baking pan
9 x 5-inch loaf pan	=	23 x 13-centimeter loaf pan
2-quart casserole	=	2-liter casserole

An International Dessert Table

Dessert is often part of a festive occasion, whether it's a birthday, a family get-together, or a holiday. You can set the table to create an atmosphere that reflects the special mood of the occasion. If you're making Chinese New Year's Cake, decorate the table with red paper (or a red paper tablecloth) and pass out red packets of *lai see*, or "lucky money." For a Christmas dessert, set the table with Christmas dishes, candles, and other fitting decorations. If you're making a fancy cake for a tea party or birthday, serve the dessert on a pretty cake plate and put a vase of freshly cut flowers on the table. If your dessert is from an Asian country such as Thailand, invite your guests to use chopsticks. When you're serving fruit, choose a variety of colors and cut the fruits into varying shapes in a pleasing arrangement on a decorative platter. Add a few flowers for even more color. Use your creativity. Most important, take the time to enjoy preparing and serving your sweet creation!

In China red is the color of happiness. A Chinese New Year's Cake topped with red dates sitting on a table decorated in red is sure to please guests. (Recipe on pages 60–61.)

A Dessert Menu

Have fun by treating your friends and family to a dessert buffet with recipes from around the world. Experiment with different themes, such as chocolate recipes from different countries or several international dishes that all use apples. Below are suggestions for two different international dessert menus, along with shopping lists of the items necessary to prepare these meals.

INTERNATIONAL DESSERT SPREAD

Moroccan date cake

Rice pudding

Honey cake

Fried bananas with cinnamon sugar

SHOPPING LIST:

Produce

4 bananas

Dairy/Egg

butter
6 eggs
5½ cups milk
whipping cream

Bottled/Boxed

vanilla extract
baking soda
honey
raisins
jam

Miscellaneous

sugar
baking powder
unbleached white flour
cinnamon
nutmeg
ground cloves
1 cup pitted, chopped dates
½ cup chopped walnuts
cardamom powder
short-grain rice
almonds, whole and sliced
pistachios
brown sugar
all-purpose flour

TEATIME TREATS

Lamingtons

Double chocolate
walnut biscotti

Cinnamon cookies

Dairy/Egg

2 eggs
butter
margarine

Canned/Bottled/Boxed

1 2-layer size package yellow
   cake mix
baking soda
vanilla extract

Miscellaneous

all-purpose flour
unbleached white flour
sugar
powdered sugar
unsweetened cocoa powder
cinnamon
salt
3 c. (24 oz.) shredded
   coconut
1 c. (8 oz.) walnuts
6 oz. (¾ c.) semisweet
   chocolate chips

Africa

Africa is a vast continent with more than fifty countries, hundreds of languages, and a wide array of cultures, both traditional and modern. The great Sahara Desert divides the continent both geographically and culturally. The countries north of the Sahara—referred to as North Africa—have many customs and traditions in common with the countries of the Middle East. In both of these regions, Islam is the main religion, and almost everyone speaks Arabic.

In North Africa, desserts are common and include a variety of pastries, cakes, and fruit dishes. By contrast, in the African countries south of the Sahara, dessert is not a typical part of most meals. Plain fruit or a fruit salad—sometimes called the "after-chop"—may be served after a meal. A wide variety of tropical fruits are grown in Africa, so there's a good selection. Other sweet snacks are made with common African ingredients such as peanuts, yams, and coconut.

This colorful African fruit salad uses a variety of fruits that are common in West African countries. (Recipe on page 30.)

African Fruit Salad (West Africa)

This is a refreshing, low-fat dessert that's a common finishing touch at dinner parties in West Africa.

1 large papaya

2 mangoes

1 large pineapple (fresh, or canned, chopped pineapple)

2 large bananas

* You can make this salad up to 4 hours before you serve it. Cover the bowl with plastic wrap and refrigerate. Add the bananas just before serving, however, or they will turn brown. To vary the recipe, you can also use fruits such as guava, melon, orange, peach, pear, and tangerine.

1. Cut papaya in half and scoop out seeds. Peel the halves. Cut the flesh into ½-inch pieces and place in a large serving bowl.

2. Peel the mangoes. Slice as much of the flesh off the pit as possible, being careful to catch any juices. Cut the flesh into ½-inch pieces. Add the pieces and their juices to the serving bowl.

3. Using a sturdy, sharp knife, cut top and bottom off pineapple. (You may need to ask an adult to help you with this.) Working from top to bottom, slice off dark, prickly outside skin. Cut out any remaining "eyes" or dark spots. Cut pineapple lengthwise into quarters. Cut each quarter lengthwise again to remove the tough inner core. Cut pineapple into 1-inch squares, again keeping the juices. Add pineapple and juices to other fruits. Toss well, cover, and refrigerate until well chilled, about 30 minutes.

4. Just before serving, peel bananas and cut into ¼-inch slices. Add to bowl, toss well, and serve.

Preparation time: 30 minutes, plus 30 minutes chilling time
Serves 8

Moroccan Date Cake

½ c. (1 stick) butter

½ c. sugar

4 eggs

1 tsp. baking powder

1 c. unbleached white flour

1 tsp. cinnamon

1 tsp. nutmeg

½ tsp. ground cloves

½ c. milk

½ tsp. vanilla extract

1 c. pitted, chopped dates

½ c. chopped walnuts

whipping cream

1. Preheat the oven to 325°F. Butter and flour a 9-inch cake pan.

2. Cream together butter and sugar. With a spoon, beat in eggs one at a time, mixing well.

3. Combine baking powder, flour, cinnamon, nutmeg, and cloves. Add dry ingredients to egg mixture, beating well.

4. Mix in milk and vanilla. Beat well. Add chopped dates and walnuts and stir to distribute them evenly.

5. Pour batter into prepared cake pan. Bake for about 30 minutes, until a knife inserted into the center comes out clean.

6. Serve with fresh whipped cream.

Preparation time: 25 minutes
Baking time: 30 minutes
Serves 8 to 10

*To reduce the fat in this recipe, use
2 percent or skim milk instead of whole milk.
You can also substitute margarine for the butter
and dairy topping for the whipped cream.*

Peanut Puffs / Mtedza (Malawi)

Malawi is known as the "warm heart of Africa" because of the friendliness of the Malawian people. African cookies or biscuits are often made in a pan over an open fire, but in this recipe they're baked in an oven.

½ c. margarine

2 tbsp. sugar

¾ c. finely chopped peanuts

½ tsp. vanilla extract

1 c. flour

powdered sugar

1. Preheat the oven to 325°F. Grease a baking sheet with cooking oil spray or a small amount of margarine.

2. Cream margarine and sugar in a medium mixing bowl.

3. Add peanuts, vanilla, and flour. Mix well. Using your fingers, roll dough into small balls, about 1 inch across.

4. Place the balls on greased baking sheet. Bake for 35 minutes.

5. Remove from oven. While still warm, roll puffs in powdered sugar. Roll in sugar again when puffs are cool.

Preparation time: 45 minutes
Baking time: 35 minutes
Makes about 2 dozen

Asia and Australia

In many Asian countries, including China, Japan, and Thailand, people eat very few desserts, though sweet snacks may be eaten between meals. In China pastries and sweet dishes are made for holidays and festivals but are rarely served with the daily meal. In many Asian countries, guests are offered a choice of assorted fruits at the end of a meal. In Thailand a fruit platter is often served for holidays. In a traditional Thai art, fruits are carved into beautiful shapes such as flowers and temples.

Desserts are more common in India, where sugarcane has been cultivated for hundreds of years. Indian desserts make use of local ingredients such as mangoes, pistachios, rice, cheese, and a variety of spices, the heart of Indian cooking.

Australian cooking is influenced by both Asia and Europe, especially England. As in England, Australians enjoy a variety of cakes and biscuits at teatime. Two favorite "Aussie" cakes are lamingtons and Pavlova, a light, airy cake named after the Russian ballerina Anna Pavlova.

Eating mango on sticky rice makes any day feel like summer. (Recipe on pages 38–39.)

Rice Pudding / Kheer (India)

Many versions of rice pudding, or kheer, are made throughout India and also in many Middle Eastern countries. In southern India, cooks serve a similar sweetened rice dish called pongal to commemorate the rice harvest festival.

⅓ c. short-grain rice

5 to 7 almonds, blanched*

5 to 7 pistachios, blanched*

5 c. milk**

½ c. sugar

¼ tsp. cardamom powder

*To blanch almonds or pistachios, put them in a bowl, pour boiling water over them, and let them sit for just a minute. Drain, then rub off the skins. You can also buy nuts that have been blanched.

**To reduce the fat in this recipe, use 2 percent or skim milk rather than whole milk.

1. Wash rice by placing it in a large saucepan and covering it with water. Drain water, being careful not to let rice float out. Repeat this process one more time. Then soak rice in water for 20 minutes.

2. Drain water and set rice aside.

3. Chop almonds and pistachios. Set aside.

4. In a large saucepan, heat half the milk over medium-high heat. Add rice and stir until the mixture boils.

5. Reduce heat and continue cooking the rice until almost all the milk is absorbed.

6. Add remaining milk, sugar, cardamom, pistachios, and almonds. Bring mixture back to a boil, stirring gently but continuously until pudding is thick and creamy.

7. Serve hot or cold.

Preparation time: 1 hour
Serves 5

Mango on Sticky Rice/
Kow Neuw Mamuang (Thailand)

Mango on sticky rice is a traditional summer dessert in Thailand because mangoes are in season then.

1 c. sticky rice

1¼ c. warm water

1 c. coconut milk*

2 tbsp. sugar

2 pinches salt

1 ripe mango

1. Place sticky rice in a microwavable bowl and cover rice with 1¼ c. warm water. Let rice soak for 10 minutes.

2. Cover the bowl with a dish or plate and cook in microwave at full power for 3 minutes. Then stir rice. Some of the rice may be cooked (it will look clearer) and some will still have a white center (the uncooked portion).

3. Heat rice in microwave for another 3 minutes. Check to see if it is done. When cooked, all the rice should be translucent. If it needs more cooking, continue to heat it and check it every 3 minutes. The exact cooking time varies from one microwave to another.

4. When rice is done, heat coconut milk in a saucepan over medium heat. Stirring constantly, let coconut milk simmer. Do not let it come to a rolling boil.

5. Add sugar and salt and stir to mix. Remove from heat.

6. Pour three-fourths of the hot coconut milk over the hot sticky rice. Let it sit for 5 minutes. The sticky rice will absorb all coconut milk. The rice should be a little mushy.

7. Peel and slice mango.

8. Place sticky rice on a small plate and top with sliced mango. Spoon remaining coconut milk on top of the rice.

Preparation time: 40 minutes
Serves 2

To reduce the fat in this recipe, use light coconut milk.

Lamingtons (Australia)

These popular cakes are named in honor of Baroness Lamington, wife of an Australian governor in the early 1900s. The cakes are a favorite with Australian children, especially for birthdays.

Cake:

1 (two-layer size) package of yellow
    cake mix

Icing:

3 c. powdered sugar

⅓ c. cocoa

3 tbsp. butter or margarine, melted

½ c. boiling water

3 c. shredded coconut

1. Bake 9 x 13-inch cake as directed on the package. Cool on a wire rack.

2. Trim crusts off cooled cake. Cut into 12 2½-inch squares.

3. Sift powdered sugar and cocoa into a bowl. Add melted butter or margarine and boiling water. Mix well with a spoon until smooth.

4. Fill a medium-sized saucepan one-fourth full of water. Simmer water and remove from stove. Put the icing bowl in saucepan.

5. Place coconut in a shallow bowl next to the saucepan. Next to the coconut, place a wire rack, so that you have an "assembly line."

6. Using two forks, dip each square of cake into warm icing. Let excess icing drip off. Then put the icing-covered cake in the coconut. Using two other forks, roll cake in coconut to cover it on all sides. Place iced, coconut-covered lamingtons on the wire rack.

7. After all cakes are iced, put them in a cool place until icing hardens.

Preparation time: 1½ hours
Makes 12 individual cakes

Europe

Desserts are practically an art form in Europe, where bakers are famous for their rich tortes and cakes, delicate pastries, soufflés, puddings, and other delectable creations. You can walk down the street in any European town and find a pastry shop or bakery filled with mouthwatering temptations. Some of the world's best-known desserts, such as apple strudel, Sacher torte, and chocolate mousse, originated in European countries. Europeans who settled in the Americas, the Caribbean, and Mexico brought their dessert traditions with them, blending Old World recipes with New World ingredients such as chocolate and tropical fruits.

Sacher torte is a rich Austrian dessert consisting of two layers of chocolate cake separated by apricot jam and covered with chocolate frosting. (Recipe on pages 48–49.)

Yogurt Pie/ Yiaourtopita (Greece)

The art of cooking has flourished in Greece for thousands of years. The world's first cookbook is said to have been written in 350 B.C. by the Greek philosopher Archestratus. Because Greece is located between western Europe and the Middle East, Greek cooking reflects the influences of both areas. Honey is a favorite sweetener, and it is often used in pastries such as baklava. This yogurt pie contains much less fat and sugar than baklava has. The ricotta cheese and yogurt in the recipe are excellent sources of calcium. The pie is delicious topped with fresh fruit, such as blueberries or strawberries.

Crust:

1¼ c. graham cracker crumbs

¼ c. sugar

¼ c. softened butter or margarine

1 tsp. cinnamon

Filling:

12 oz. ricotta or farmer cheese

1½ c. plain yogurt

3 tbsp. honey

1 tsp. vanilla extract

1. Preheat oven to 375°F.

2. Combine graham cracker crumbs, sugar, butter, and cinnamon in a mixing bowl. Mix well with a spoon. Press the mixture evenly into a 9-inch pie pan.

3. Bake crust for 5 to 10 minutes, then cool.

4. By hand or with an electric mixer, beat ricotta or farmer cheese well, then add yogurt a little at a time, mixing well. Stir in honey and vanilla.

5. Pour filling into pie shell and refrigerate for at least 24 hours before serving.

Preparation time: 25 minutes
Chilling time: 24 hours
Serves 8

*To make a low-fat version of this pie, choose part-skim ricotta cheese and nonfat or low-fat yogurt. Use margarine instead of butter.

Honey Cake/Kovrizhka Medovaya (Russia)

Honey cake used to be served during religious holiday celebrations in Russia. It's become a common dessert that is especially popular with children.

2 eggs

½ c. brown sugar

2 c. all-purpose flour

½ tsp. baking soda

1 c. honey

½ c. raisins

½ c. sliced almonds (or other nuts)

1. Preheat oven to 350°F. Grease and flour a 9 x 5-inch loaf pan.

2. With a fork, beat eggs thoroughly in a small bowl. Add sugar and stir well.

3. Pour flour into a large mixing bowl. Add egg mixture and baking soda and stir well.

4. Add honey and mix for 5 minutes. Stir in raisins.

5. Pour dough into pan and spread evenly. Sprinkle with nuts.

6. Bake for 50 to 60 minutes, or until toothpick stuck in the middle of the cake comes out clean. Cool cake in pan for 10 minutes, then remove and cool on wire rack. Serve cake with whipped cream or jam.

Preparation time: 25 minutes
Baking time: 50 to 60 minutes
Makes 9 to 12 pieces

Double Chocolate Walnut Biscotti (Italy)

These crunchy hard cookies are perfect for dunking in coffee, tea, or hot chocolate. Biscotti means "twice cooked"—the secret of their crunch!

2 c. all-purpose flour

½ c. unsweetened cocoa powder

1 tsp. baking soda

1 tsp. salt

6 tbsp. (¾ stick) unsalted butter, softened

1 c. sugar

2 large eggs

1 c. walnuts, chopped

¾ c. semisweet chocolate chips

1. Preheat oven to 350°F. Butter and flour a large baking sheet.

2. In a bowl, whisk together flour, cocoa powder, baking soda, and salt.

3. In another bowl, use an electric mixer to beat together butter and sugar until light and fluffy. Add eggs and beat until well combined. Stir in flour mixture to form a stiff dough. Stir in walnuts and chocolate chips.

4. On prepared baking sheet, and with floured hands, form dough into two slightly flattened logs, each 12 inches long and 2 inches wide.

5. Bake logs 35 minutes, or until slightly firm to the touch. Cool on baking sheet 15 minutes.

6. Transfer logs to a cutting board. Cut logs diagonally into ¾-inch slices.

7. Arrange biscotti, cut sides down, on baking sheet and bake until crisp, about 10 minutes. Cool biscotti on a rack. They will keep in air-tight containers for a week.

Preparation time: 90 minutes
Makes 30 biscotti

Sacher Torte (Austria)

Created in 1832 by apprentice baker Franz Sacher for an Austrian prince, this chocolate cake soon gained popularity. Sacher's descendants later built and operated the Sacher Hotel in Vienna and made the cake their specialty. When a popular Viennese pastry shop copied the recipe, the Sachers took them to court. In the court decision, the Sachers retained the right to use the name "Original Sacher torte."

Cake:

5⅓ oz. bittersweet chocolate

1 stick plus 3 tbsp. butter, melted

½ c. sugar

6 eggs, separated*

1 tbsp. powdered sugar

1 tbsp. baking powder

1 c. flour

12 oz. apricot jam at room temperature

Chocolate icing:

7 oz. bittersweet chocolate

1 c. powdered sugar

2 tbsp. butter

A few drops fresh lemon juice

8 to 10 tbsp. hot water

1. Prepare a 9-inch springform pan by cutting waxed paper the exact size of the base of the pan, plus a 29 x 2¼-inch strip for the sides. (Measure the circle for the base by putting the pan on top of the waxed paper and drawing a circle around it.) Insert waxed paper in pan.

2. Preheat oven to 325°F.

3. In a double boiler, heat chocolate until melted.

4. In a large bowl, beat butter and sugar using an electric mixer. Add melted chocolate. Then add egg yolks, one at a time, beating continuously to make a creamy mixture.

5. In another bowl, using clean beaters, beat egg whites and powdered sugar until stiff peaks form.

6. Add egg whites to chocolate mixture, then sift baking powder and flour together onto egg whites, a little at a time. Fold egg whites and flour carefully into chocolate mixture.

7. Pour batter into prepared pan, using a spatula to spread it evenly. Bake for about 50 minutes. Test for doneness by inserting a toothpick into cake. If the toothpick comes out clean, the cake is done.

8. Remove cake from oven, remove springform rim, carefully peel off side paper, and allow cake to cool slightly.

9. Turn cake onto a cake plate and remove base of pan and waxed paper. Slice cake horizontally into two halves. Spread bottom layer with jam and replace top layer.

10. To make icing, melt chocolate in a double boiler. Add powdered sugar, butter, lemon juice, and 1 tbsp. of hot water at a time to get right consistency for spreading on cake.

11. While icing is still hot, spread over top and sides of cake and allow icing to cool completely.

12. Serve cake with whipped cream, if desired.

Preparation time: 30 to 45 minutes
Baking time: about 50 minutes
Serves 12

To separate an egg, crack it cleanly on the edge of a non-plastic bowl. Holding the two halves of the eggshell over the bowl, gently pour the egg yolk back and forth between the two halves, letting the egg white drip into the bowl and being careful not to break the yolk.

The Caribbean, Mexico, and South America

The cuisine of the Caribbean islands, Mexico, and the Americas is a diverse blend of foods that reflects the tastes and traditions of the various people who have lived in these regions, including many native tribes, the Spanish, the English, and others. The Europeans brought the tradition of using dairy products, eggs, and sugar in desserts, while the indigenous, or native people, contributed a variety of fruits, as well as chocolate.

In the Caribbean islands, dessert is more likely to be a piece of fresh fruit than a rich concoction. The islands offer a huge variety of fruit, from pineapples and bananas to mangoes, papayas, and custard apples, large fruits with spiky skin and white flesh. In Mexico and South America, people enjoy a wide variety of desserts, including cookies, flan (milk pudding), cakes, and sweet breads.

Preparing Caribbean sorbet is a great way to cool down on a hot summer day. (Recipe on page 54.)

Cinnamon Cookies/
Polvorones de Canela (Mexico)

Polvorones are small shortbread cookies. They may be flavored with cinnamon or orange and are often made with ground nuts. They are great with Mexican hot chocolate.

1 c. (2 sticks) butter, softened

½ c. powdered sugar

½ tsp. cinnamon

¼ tsp. salt

1 tsp. vanilla extract

2 c. unbleached white flour

For rolling:

1 c. powdered sugar

1 tsp. cinnamon

1. With an electric mixer, combine butter and sugar to make a smooth, creamy mixture. Add cinnamon, salt, and vanilla. Fold in flour, making a stiff dough. Chill for an hour or two.

2. When you're ready to bake the cookies, preheat the oven to 350°F. Butter a baking sheet.

3. Form the dough into 1-inch balls.

4. Mix together 1 c. powdered sugar and 1 tsp. cinnamon. Roll the balls in the cinnamon-sugar mixture.

5. Bake the cookies for 15 to 20 minutes, until nicely browned. Cool on a wire rack.

Preparation time: 20 minutes
Chilling time: 1–2 hours
Baking time: 15–20 minutes
Makes about 30 cookies

Caribbean Sorbet (The Caribbean Islands)

This sweet and icy sorbet is a perfect dessert for a hot Caribbean night.

2 very ripe bananas, frozen, peeled, and sliced

3 oz. fresh pineapple juice

3 oz. frozen pineapple juice

2 tbsp. unsweetened shredded coconut

1. Place frozen banana slices, fresh and frozen pineapple juice, and coconut in a blender or food processor. Puree until mixture is smooth and resembles soft ice cream or a slush.

2. Serve immediately in chilled bowls.

Preparation time: 15 minutes
Serves 4

Fried Bananas with Cinnamon Sugar/Banana Frita com Canela e Açúcar (Brazil)

Brazilians eat fried bananas either with a meal or as dessert with cinnamon and sugar.

4 bananas

2 tbsp. butter or margarine

2 tbsp. sugar

½ tsp. cinnamon

1. Peel bananas and cut them in half lengthwise.

2. In a frying pan, melt butter or margarine. Fry bananas on one side until golden brown, about 5 minutes. Turn them and fry on other side until golden brown.

3. While bananas are frying, mix sugar and cinnamon in a small bowl.

4. With a spatula, remove bananas and place on serving platter. Sprinkle with cinnamon sugar mixture and serve hot.

Preparation time: 5 minutes
Cooking time: 10 minutes
Serves 4

Flan/Quesillo de Leche (Venezuela)

Flan, or milk pudding, is a favorite dessert throughout Mexico, Central America, and South America.

3 eggs

1 14-ounce can sweetened
    condensed milk

3 c. milk

2 tsp. vanilla extract

1 c. sugar

**To make a low-fat version of a
traditional flan, substitute 2 percent
milk for the condensed milk and
the whole milk.*

1. Preheat oven to 400°F.

2. With a hand mixer or fork, lightly beat eggs.

3. Add condensed and regular milk* and vanilla and blend well. Set aside.

4. Heat sugar over medium-high heat in a small saucepan, stirring constantly, until the sugar carmelizes (turns brown and syrupy). This may take 20 minutes.

5. Quickly pour carmelized sugar into bottom of ovenproof 2-quart mold or bowl, coating bottom and sides of container. Place mold in shallow pan of cold water—water should reach halfway to three-fourths of the way up side of the mold.

6. Pour custard mixture into the mold.

7. Bake for 1 hour on middle rack of oven, until flan appears golden brown on top.

8. Refrigerate 12 hours or overnight.

9. When you're ready to serve the flan, turn it onto a platter. The flan will be covered with a caramel sauce.

Preparation and cooking time: 1 hour 20 minutes
Chilling time: 12 hours
Serves 6

Holiday and Festival Desserts

People around the world celebrate holidays and festivals with sweet foods. For many people, baking and preparing special desserts is a cherished part of the holiday season. Cooks from points as far north as the Arctic Circle in Norway to the southern tip of Chile may spend weeks baking Christmas breads, cookies, and other treats. In India many family members might gather together to prepare a dozen or more sweets for Diwali, the joyful festival of lights that commemorates the Hindu god Rama's return to his kingdom after a fourteen-year exile. Homes are decorated, sweets are distributed to everyone, and lamps are lit. Similarly, in Muslim homes, cooks spend hours making a variety of foods to celebrate Eid al-Fitr, the end of the holy month of Ramadan. After a month of fasting during the day, families gather for a great feast, including desserts such as stuffed pancakes covered in syrup.

The recipes in this section offer a sampling of desserts served on special occasions in different countries. Start with these recipes, then discover others to get an international taste of the holidays.

During Eid al-Fitr, Lebanese Muslims feast on delights such as these pancakes stuffed with nuts, cinnamon, and sugar. (Recipe on pages 68–69.)

Chinese New Year's Cake

People in China generally eat few desserts. Usually they end a meal with fresh fruit. Pastries and sweet dishes are made in China, but they are special festival foods and are rarely served with the daily meal. This traditional cake is served for Chinese New Year. Red dates, the color of happiness and celebration, add a festive touch to the cake. Sometimes called jujubes, these dates can be found dried at most supermarkets or specialty stores.

4 to 5 Chinese dried red dates

11 oz. brown candy (about 5 slabs)

2 c. water, boiling

7 c. glutinous rice flour

white sesame seeds to garnish
   (optional)

1. Soak dried dates in cold water until soft, about 30 minutes. Remove from water and cut into halves, removing the pits. Set aside.

2. Cut each slab of brown candy into two or three pieces and place in a glass or metal mixing bowl. Carefully add 2 c. boiling water and let candy dissolve and cool.

3. Place glutinous rice flour in a large bowl. Make a hollow in the center of the flour and pour the cooled, dissolved sugar (brown candy) into the hollow. Stir flour and sugar together.

4. When a dough begins to form, use your hands to knead it gently. If necessary, add cold water 1 tbsp. at a time until dough is smooth and shiny.

5. Lightly grease an 8-inch round cake pan with vegetable oil. Place dough in pan and mold it to fill the pan.

6. Decorate the top of the cake with dates. Sprinkle sesame seeds over all, if desired.

7. Place pan in the rack of a steamer,* cover, and steam over high heat until cake begins to pull away from the sides of the pan, about 35 to 50 minutes. While steaming, check the water level. Add more if necessary.

8. Remove cake from steamer. Pour off any water that has collected on top of the cake. Set aside to cool. When completely cool, run a knife along the edge of the cake and turn it out of the pan. Wrap loosely in plastic wrap and refrigerate until ready to eat. (Cake is best if eaten the day after cooking.)

9. To serve, cut cake into small slices (not wedges). Serve at room temperature, or warm up by resteaming pieces on a plate.

Preparation time: 45 minutes
Steaming time: 45 to 60 minutes
Makes 1 8-inch round cake

*If you don't have a steamer, improvise by using common kitchen items. Place two heatproof glass mugs or a large tin can upside down in the bottom of a large pot with a tight-fitting lid. Fill with water up to about three-quarters of the height of the mugs or can. Carefully set a dinner plate on the mugs or can. The plate should not touch the inside of the pot. Place whatever is being steamed on the plate, place the lid on the pot, and bring water to a boil. As with a regular steamer, be sure to check the water level regularly and refill as necessary.

Haman's Ears or Haman's Pockets/ Hamantaschen (Israel)

Dough:

⅔ c. butter

½ c. sugar

l egg

½ tsp. vanilla extract

2½ to 3 c. sifted unbleached all-purpose flour

l tsp. baking powder

dash of salt

Fruit filling:

¾ c. pitted prunes

⅓ c. seedless raisins

¼ c. water

¼ c. shelled walnuts

¼ apple with peel

juice and rind of ¼ lemon*

2 tbsp. sugar

1. Mix butter and sugar until smooth and creamy. Add egg and beat until smooth.

2. Add vanilla. Stir in sifted flour, baking powder, and salt until a ball of dough is formed.

3. Chill 2 to 3 hours or overnight.

4. For fruit filling, simmer prunes and raisins in water, covered, for 15 minutes, or until prunes soften slightly. Add nuts and apple. Grind or chop in a food processor. Add lemon juice and rind and sugar. Mix well. Refrigerate until ready to use.

5. Preheat oven to 375°F. Generously grease 2 cookie sheets.

6. Roll out ¼ of dough on a lightly floured board until ⅛-inch thick. With a cookie cutter or the rim of a glass, cut dough into 2-inch circles. Place 1 tsp. filling in the center of each circle.

7. Slightly moisten the rim of the circles with water. Pull the edges of the dough up to form a triangle around the filling and pinch the three corners together.

8. Bake on a cookie sheet 10 to 15 minutes, or until the tops are golden.

Preparation time: 45 minutes
Chilling time: 2 to 3 hours
Baking time: 10 to 15 minutes
Makes about 36 cookies

*Use a potato peeler or a zester to gently remove peel in small strips from the lemon. Try to avoid getting the white part, which has a bitter taste. Chop or mince the peel with a knife for even smaller pieces.

Christmas Bread/ *Pan de Navidad (Chile)*

This is a traditional bread made for Christmas in Chile. Employers often give their workers a package containing Christmas bread and a bottle of wine.

4 c. unbleached white flour

1 c. sugar

1 c. (about 6 oz.) diced dried assorted fruits (peaches, pears, apples, raisins, prunes, apricots, dates, currants)

½ c. chopped almonds

½ c. chopped walnuts

1 tsp. cinnamon

pinch of ground cloves

½ tsp. nutmeg

2 eggs, beaten

2 tbsp. butter or margarine, melted

¾ to 1 c. milk

sugar for sprinkling

1. Preheat oven to 350°F. Butter a 10-inch pie plate.

2. Sift flour and sugar into a bowl. Add fruits, nuts, cinnamon, cloves, and nutmeg. Stir until mixed.

3. Lightly beat eggs. Melt butter. Fold eggs, melted butter, and milk into flour mixture. If batter seems too thick, add a little extra milk.

4. Smooth batter into pie plate. Sprinkle a bit of sugar on top and bake for 1 hour.

Preparation time: 45 minutes
Baking time: 1 hour
Serves 8

*Reduce the fat in this recipe by using margarine and skim milk.

Strawberry Torte / Jordgubbstårta (Sweden)

To Swedes, Midsummer would not be Midsummer without strawberries, a symbol of the summer solstice and the return of the light. Strawberries are the favorite dessert for this festive holiday. They may be served alone with sugar and whipped cream, with vanilla ice cream, or in this tasty torte.

Cake:*

4 tbsp. butter

1¼ c. sifted cake flour

1½ tsp. baking powder

2 large eggs

¾ c. sugar

1 tsp. vanilla extract or the zest of 1 lemon

½ c. milk or water

Icing:

8 oz. heavy cream

1 pt. fresh or frozen (thawed, drained, hulled, and sliced) strawberries

6 tbsp. strawberry jam

To save time, you can use packaged white or yellow cake mix.

1. Preheat oven to 350°F.

2. Prepare a 9-inch springform pan by cutting waxed paper the exact size of the base of the pan, plus a 29 x 2¼-inch strip for the sides. (Measure the circle for the base by putting the pan on top of the waxed paper and drawing a circle around it.) Insert waxed paper in pan.

3. Melt butter and set aside to cool.

4. Mix flour and baking powder together and set aside.

5. In a large bowl, whisk together eggs and sugar for several minutes until foamy. Add vanilla extract or lemon zest to eggs.

6. Stir milk or water into cooled melted butter.

7. Beat liquid ingredients into egg mixture, then stir in dry ingredients. Beat by hand for 1 to 2 minutes until batter is smooth. Pour batter into prepared pan.

8. Bake for about 30 minutes, until a toothpick or knife inserted into center of cake comes out clean. Cool on a rack. Gently peel off wax paper.

9. With a cake or bread knife, slice cake in half horizontally and separate the two horizontal halves.

10. For the icing, whip the cream until soft peaks form. Do not overwhip or cream will turn to butter.

11. Mix half the sliced berries with half the whipped cream.

12. Spread strawberry jam over the top of the bottom cake layer, then cover with whipped cream and berry mixture. Place the second cake layer on top of the bottom one. Frost the top and sides of cake with remaining whipped cream. Decorate top with remaining strawberries.

13. Cover lightly with plastic wrap and refrigerate until ready to serve.

Preparation time: 45 to 60 minutes
Baking time: 30 minutes
Makes 1 9-inch torte

Stuffed Pancakes/ *Atayef Mehshi* (Lebanon)

Lebanese Muslims eat these delicious pancakes on many festive occasions, especially during Ramadan and Eid al-Fitr.

Batter:*

1 envelope active dry yeast

1 tsp. sugar

1¼ to 2 c. warm water

1½ c. all-purpose flour

1 tsp. vegetable oil

Filling:

2 c. chopped walnuts

3 tbsp. sugar

2 tsp. cinnamon

Syrup:

½ tbsp. orange flower water (optional)

1 c. pancake syrup or dark corn syrup

Although the flavor and texture will not be the same, you can simplify the recipe by using any pancake batter mix instead of the yeast mixture given here.

1. Dissolve yeast and sugar in ½ c. warm water. Cover lightly with a damp cloth and leave in a warm place for about 20 minutes, or until mixture begins to foam.

2. Warm a large mixing bowl by rinsing with hot water and drying thoroughly. Sift flour into warmed bowl. Make a depression in the center, pour in yeast mixture, and beat into the flour. Continue beating, gradually adding the remaining warm water until mixture is the consistency of pancake batter. Cover mixture with a damp cloth and leave in a warm place for 1 hour, or until bubbly.

3. In a small bowl, prepare filling by mixing walnuts, sugar, and cinnamon. Set aside.

4. Preheat oven to 375°F.

5. Place vegetable oil in a heavy skillet and swirl to coat evenly. Heat pan over high heat.

6. Pour about ¼ c. batter into heated pan. Tilt pan gently to even out batter, but keep pancake fairly thick and round. Cook until it begins to bubble and comes away easily from pan. Cook only one side of pancake.

7. Use a spatula to remove pancake from pan and place pancake on a greased cookie sheet or baking pan. Put 2 tbsp. walnut filling on uncooked side of pancake and fold in half. Firmly pinch edges together to keep filling in place.

8. Repeat with remaining batter and filling, adding oil to pan as needed.

9. When all pancakes are cooked and filled, place cookie sheet or baking pan in oven and bake for 10 to 15 minutes. Remove from oven and cool slightly. Mix orange flower water, if using, with syrup. Dip pancakes in syrup mixture while they are still warm. If desired, serve with sour cream or cottage cheese.

Preparation time: 1 to 1½ hours, plus 1 hour sitting time
Baking time: 10 to 15 minutes
Serves 4 to 6

Index

Photo Acknowledgments
The photographs in this book are reproduced with the permission of: © Becky Luigart-Stayner/CORBIS, pp. 2–3; © Walter and Louiseann Pietrowicz/September 8th Stock, pp. 4 (both), 5 (both), 6, 16, 24, 28, 32, 34, 37, 41, 42, 46, 50, 52, 57, 58, 65; © Robert Fried, p. 8; © Nik Wheeler, p. 10; © Reuters NewMedia Inc./ CORBIS, p. 13; © Phil Schermeister/CORBIS, p. 14.

Cover photos: © Walter and Louiseann Pietrowicz/September 8th Stock, front top and back; © Todd Strand/Independent Picture Service, front bottom and spine.

The illustrations on pages 7, 17, 25, 29, 30, 31, 35, 36, 39, 43, 44, 49, 51, 56, 59, 61, 63, 64, 66, 68 are by Tim Seeley.